YACHT RACING RULES
the ESSENTIALS

HENK PLAATJE

Published 2005 by Adlard Coles Nautical
an imprint of A & C Black Publishers Ltd
37 Soho Square, London W1D 3QZ
www.adlardcoles.com

Copyright © Uitgeverij Hollandia BV

First published in The Netherlands 2001 by Uitgeverij Hollandia BV
First edition published in the UK by Adlard Coles Nautical 2005

ISBN 0-7136-7257-9

A CIP catalogue record for this book is available from the British Library.

Printed and bound in Italy by Legatoria Editoriale Giovanni Olivotto LEGO SpA.

Note: While all reasonable care has been taken in the publication of this book,
the publisher takes no responsibility for the use of the methods or products
described in the book.

Front cover photo courtesy of Kos Picture Source

ADLARD COLES NAUTICAL
LONDON

Contents

Key to symbols

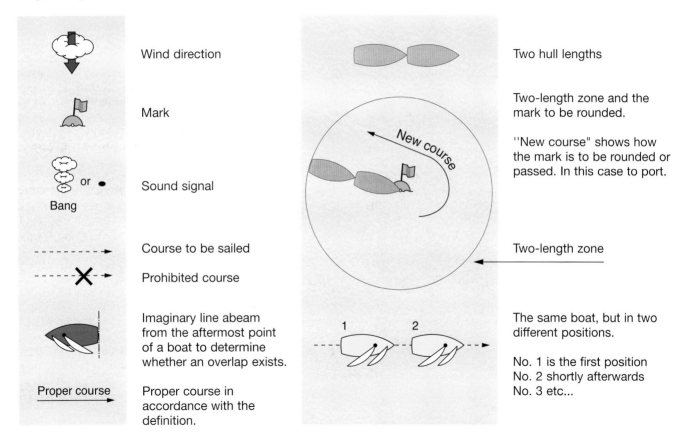

Wind direction

Mark

Sound signal

Bang

Course to be sailed

Prohibited course

Imaginary line abeam from the aftermost point of a boat to determine whether an overlap exists.

Proper course

Proper course in accordance with the definition.

Two hull lengths

Two-length zone and the mark to be rounded.

"New course" shows how the mark is to be rounded or passed. In this case to port.

New course

Two-length zone

The same boat, but in two different positions.

No. 1 is the first position
No. 2 shortly afterwards
No. 3 etc...

Introduction

The Racing Rules of Sailing 2005-2008
This guide is a simplified version of "The Racing Rules of Sailing 2005-2008" (RRS). In order to make it easier for you to understand them, the rules and definitions have in some places been adapted. For the official text you should always refer to the original book. The aim of this guide is to teach the basic rules to novice and advanced racing sailors using plenty of illustrations.

Sportsmanship and the rules
Competitors in the sport of sailing are governed by a body of rules that they are expected to follow and enforce. A fundamental principle of sportsmanship is that when competitors break a rule they will promptly take a penalty or retire.

Giving help
You must give help to any person in danger.

Wearing personal buoyancy
Sometimes you are required to wear personal buoyancy. It is sensible to wear personal buoyancy at all times.

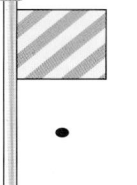

Code flag Y and one sound signal.

When code flag Y is displayed personal buoyancy must be worn.

42 Prohibited actions

While racing you may only use wind and water to increase or decrease your speed. You may adjust the trim of sails and hull, but pumping, rolling, ooching, paddling or sculling or slowing down using a paddle or a bucket are all prohibited. It is permitted to slow down using the rudder as a brake.

Preparation
Be well prepared, read the sailing instructions carefully and make sure that your boat is in mint condition.

Points of sailing and courses

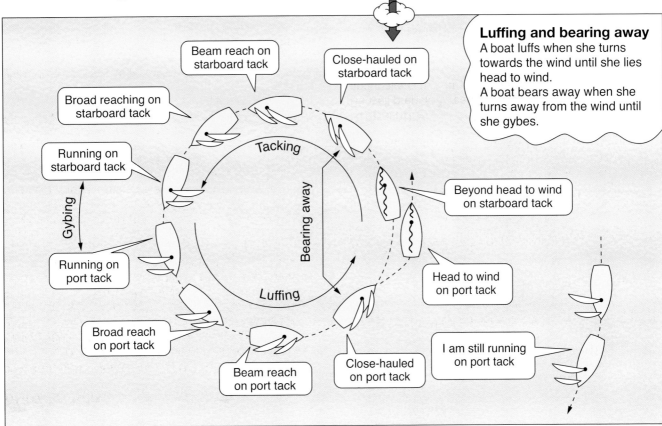

Luffing and bearing away
A boat luffs when she turns towards the wind until she lies head to wind.
A boat bears away when she turns away from the wind until she gybes.

Starting procedure

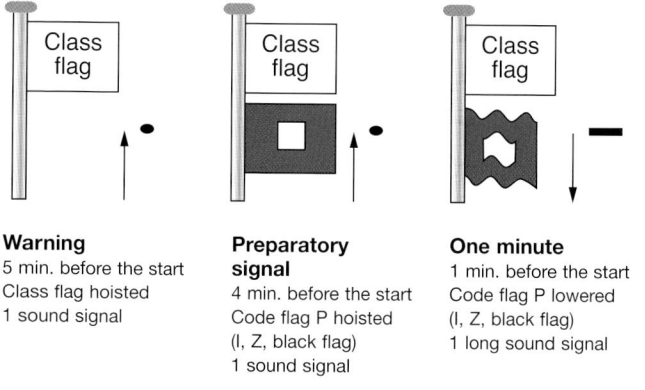

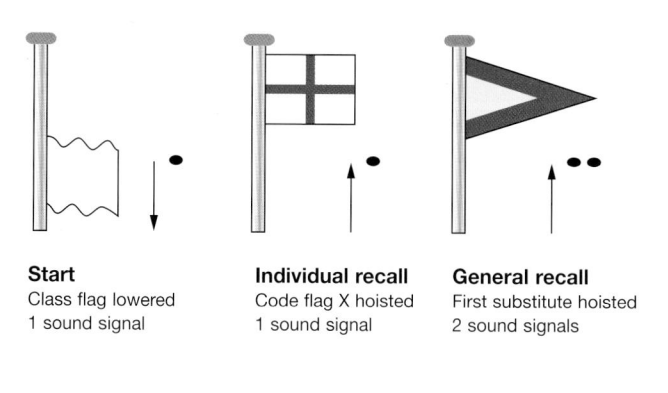

Warning
5 min. before the start
Class flag hoisted
1 sound signal

Preparatory signal
4 min. before the start
Code flag P hoisted
(I, Z, black flag)
1 sound signal

One minute
1 min. before the start
Code flag P lowered
(I, Z, black flag)
1 long sound signal

Start
Class flag lowered
1 sound signal

Individual recall
Code flag X hoisted
1 sound signal

General recall
First substitute hoisted
2 sound signals

Definition

Starting

A boat starts when, after her starting signal, any part of her hull, crew or equipment first crosses the starting line.

A has started,
B has not yet
started.

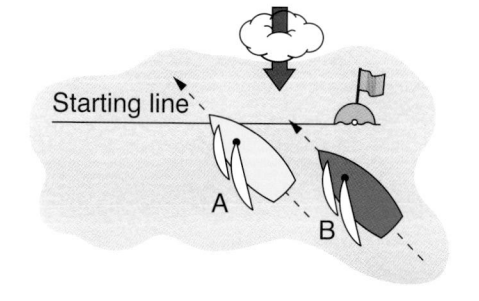

Definition

Racing

A boat is racing from her preparatory signal until she finishes and clears the finishing line.

Comment

The preparatory signal is given four minutes before the starting signal. From now on you are on your own and must not receive any help from others.

The starting procedure consists of three signals. The warning signal, the preparatory signal and the starting signal. They are all described in the sailing instructions, and may be different from the procedure outlined above.

Right of way

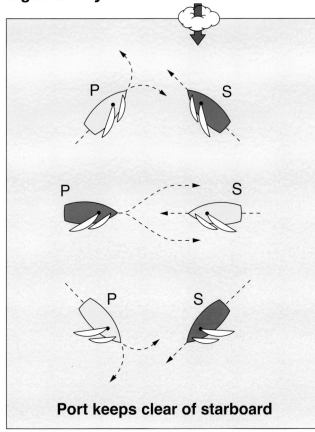

Port keeps clear of starboard

10 On opposite tacks

When boats are on opposite tacks a port-tack boat shall keep clear* of a starboard-tack boat.

Definition

On a tack, starboard or port
A boat is on the tack, starboard or port, corresponding to her windward side (for an explanation of the term windward see next page).

Comment

starboard = right
port = left

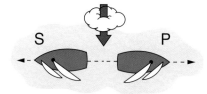

A boat is on port tack or on port (P). The mainsail lies on the right-hand side.
A boat is on starboard tack or on starboard (S). The mainsail lies on the left-hand side.

* Keeping clear roughly means: avoiding and not coming too close.

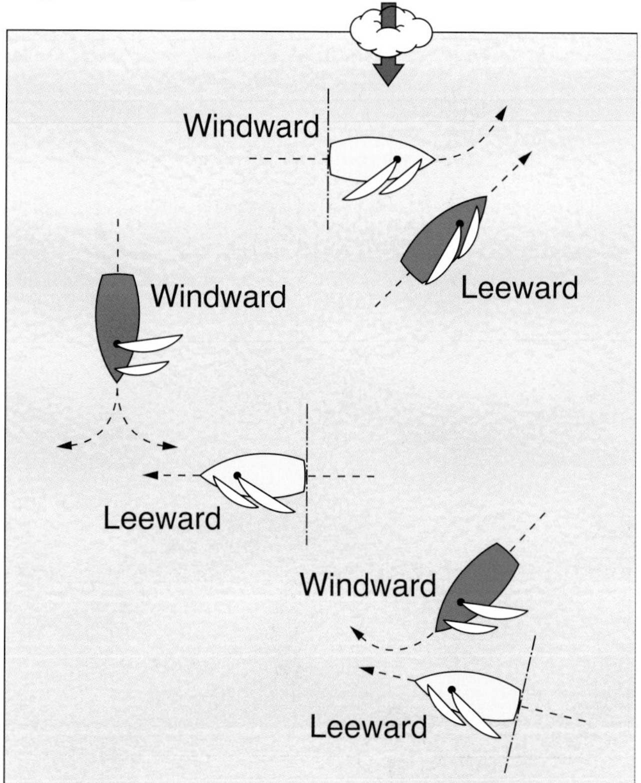

Right of way

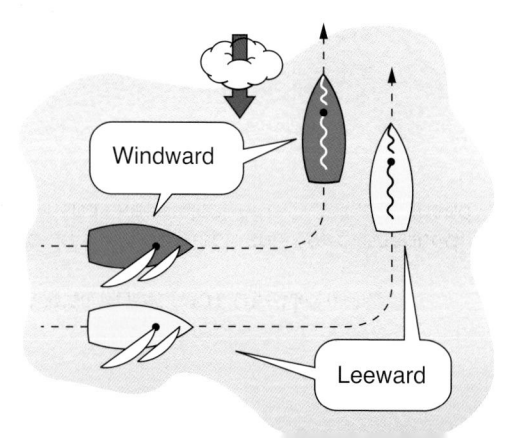

Windward keeps clear of leeward

11 On the same tack, overlapped

When boats are on the same tack and overlapped, a windward boat shall keep clear of a leeward boat.

Definition

Leeward and windward

Windward is the side where the wind comes from, the other side is leeward. When you are sailing by the lee or directly downwind, the side on which your mainsail lies is the leeward side.

Right of way

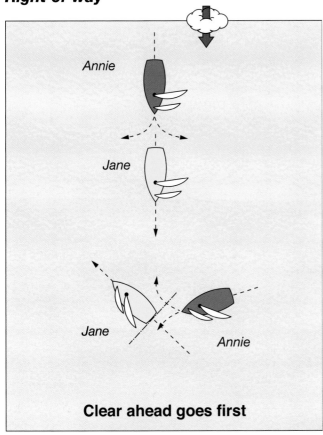

Clear ahead goes first

12 On the same tack, not overlapped

When boats are on the same tack and not overlapped, a boat clear astern shall keep clear of a boat clear ahead.

Definition

Clear astern and clear ahead; overlap
A boat is clear astern of another when she is behind a line abeam from the aftermost point of the other boat.

A is clear astern of B, C and D.
B, C and D are clear ahead of A.
B and C are overlapped, and so are C and D.
B and D are overlapped.

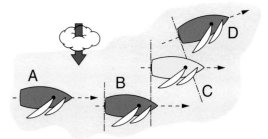

Drawing left: Annie must keep clear.

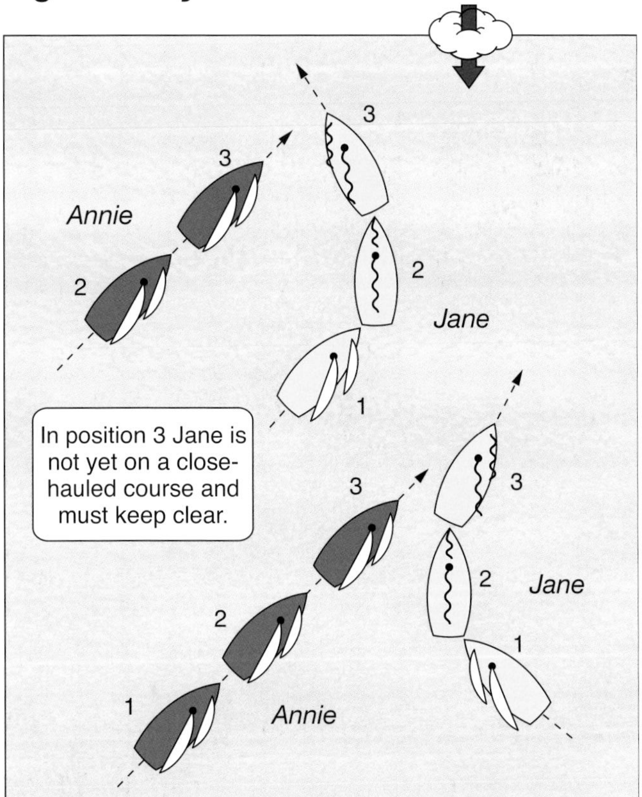

Right of way

In position 3 Jane is not yet on a close-hauled course and must keep clear.

The boat that tacks must keep clear

13 While tacking

After a boat passes head to wind, she shall keep clear of other boats until she is on a close-hauled course.

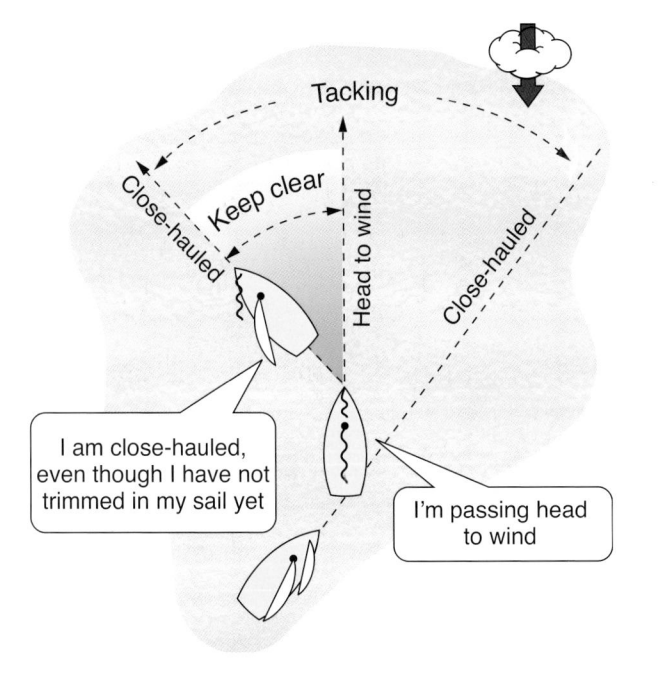

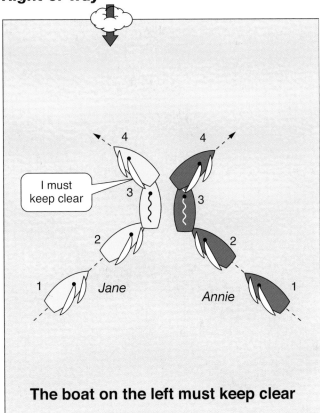

The boat on the left must keep clear

13 While tacking

After a boat passes head to wind, she shall keep clear of other boats until she is on a close-hauled course. If two boats pass head to wind at the same time, the one on the other's port side shall keep clear.

Comment

Jane and Annie are tacking simultaneously.
Jane is on Annie's port side and must keep clear.

General limitations

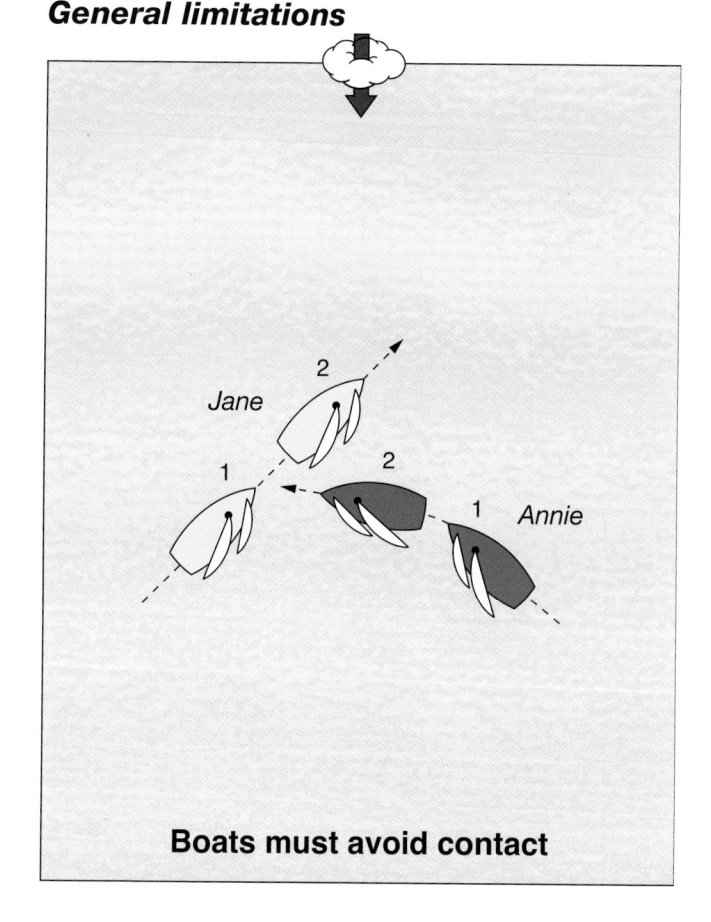

Boats must avoid contact

14 Avoiding contact

A boat shall avoid contact with another boat if reasonably possible.

However, a right-of-way boat or one entitled to room

a. need not act to avoid contact until it is clear that the other boat is not keeping clear or giving room, and
b. shall not be penalized under this rule unless there is contact that causes damage.

Comment

This means that if you are concerned that a collision may be about to occur, you are required to try to avoid that collision, even though you are the right-of-way boat.

Annie as a starboard-tack boat has right of way, but is **obliged** to change course to avoid a collision. Jane breaks a rule.

General limitations

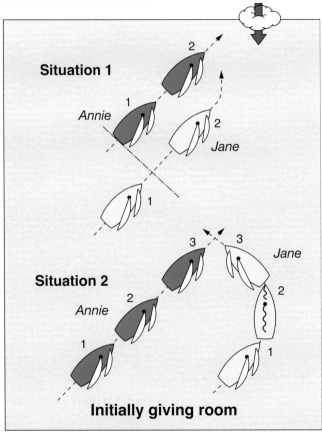

Situation 1

Annie

Jane

Situation 2

Annie

Jane

Initially giving room

15 Acquiring right of way

When a boat acquires right of way, she shall initially*
give the other boat room to keep clear, unless ... *(see
next page).*

Comment

Situation 1, position 1: Annie has right of way (clear
ahead, clear astern). In position 2 an overlap is created
and Jane acquires right of way.

Situation 2: After the tacking manoeuvre Jane acquires
right of way because she is now on starboard tack.

In both situations, if Annie does not get enough time to
avoid Jane, after Jane has acquired right of way, then
Jane breaks the rule.

* Initially here means that a boat must be given time to
  take avoiding action but that she does have the
  obligation to begin doing so **immediately**.

General limitations

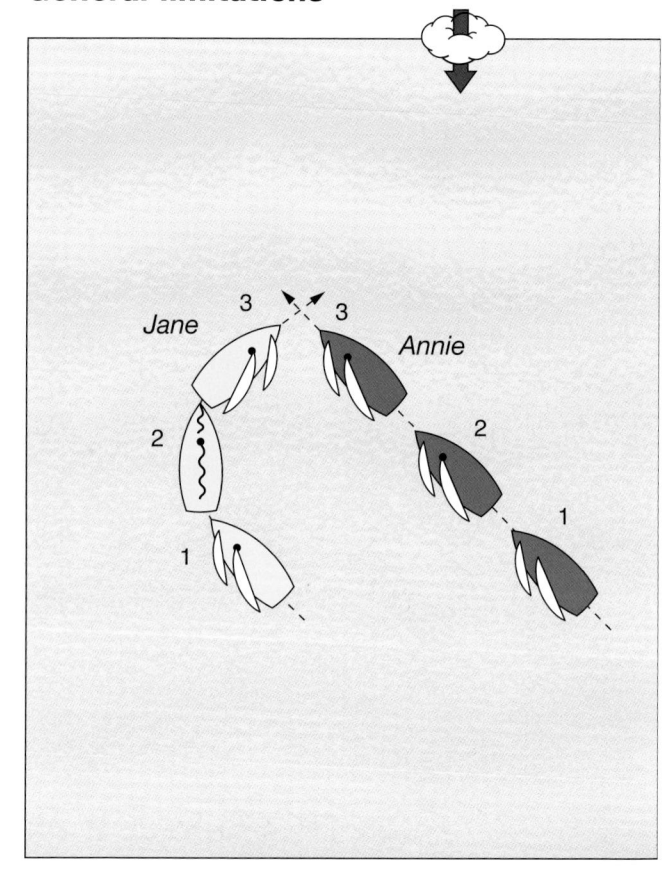

15 Acquiring right of way

…unless she acquires right of way because of the other boat's actions.

Comment

Jane is sailing on starboard tack and tacks right in front of Annie. Annie thus acquires right of way because of Jane's tacking manoeuvre.

Annie is not required to give room under this rule. She will have to take avoiding action in accordance with rule 14 – avoiding contact.

Jane breaks the rule. She may take a penalty by sailing clear as soon as possible and immediately making two turns *(see page 37)*. A two turns penalty includes two tacks and two gybes.

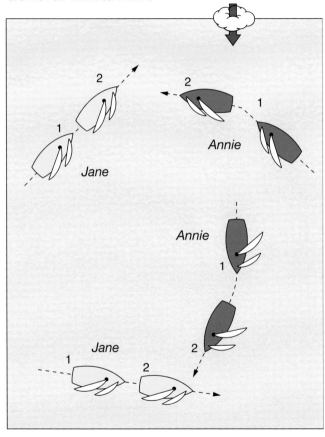

16 Changing course

When a right-of-way boat changes course, she shall give the other boat room to keep clear.

Comment

In positions 1 Jane could have crossed in front of Annie. Annie changes course, however, forcing Jane to take avoiding action.

If Jane is able to take avoiding action without too much trouble, there is no issue, but if she can barely keep clear, then Annie breaks the rule.

General limitations

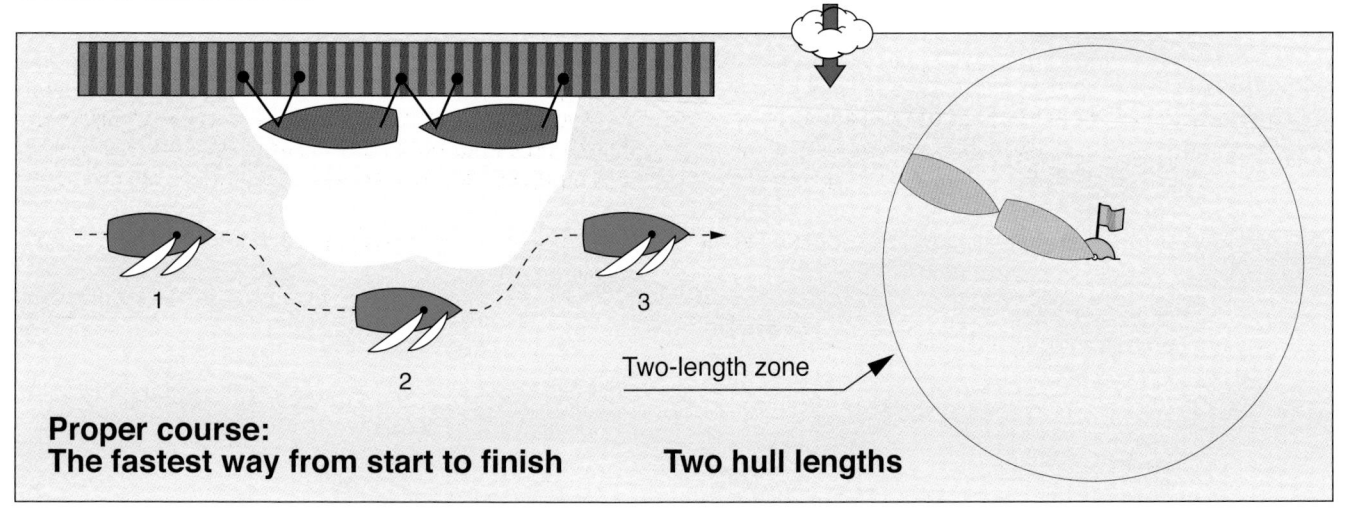

Proper course:
The fastest way from start to finish

Two-length zone

Two hull lengths

Definitions

Proper course
A course a boat would sail to finish as soon as possible in the absence of the other boats referred to in the rule.

Two-length zone
The area around a mark or obstruction within a distance of two hull lengths of the boat nearer to it.

Comments

Proper course is not the shortest course but the fastest course, so you are allowed, for example, to sail around any lulls.

Hull length refers to the bare hull without any equipment such as a rudder hung from the stern or a spinnaker.

General limitations

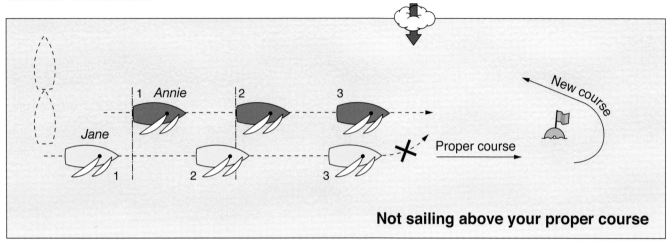

Not sailing above your proper course

17.1 On the same tack, proper course

If a boat clear astern becomes overlapped within two of her hull lengths to leeward of a boat on the same tack, she shall not sail above her proper course while they remain overlapped within that distance, unless... *(see next page).*

Comment

In position 1 Jane is clear astern. In position 2 Jane acquires an overlap to leeward.

The distance between both boats is less than two hull lengths. Now Jane must not sail higher than her proper course to the mark, because the course to the mark is her proper course.

General limitations

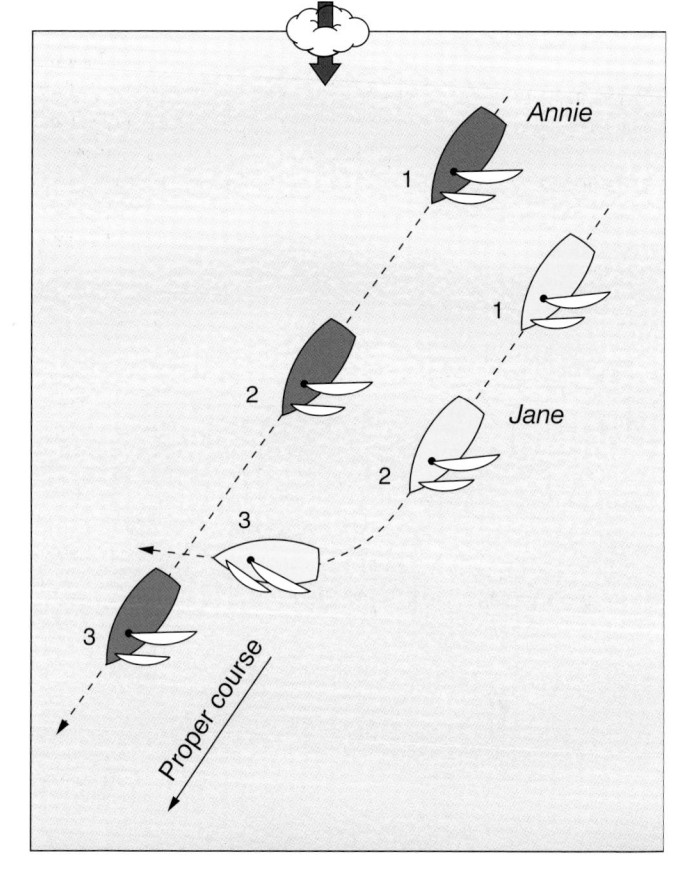

17.1 On the same tack, proper course

...unless in doing so she promptly sails astern of the other boat.

Comment

In positions 1 and 2 Jane must not sail above her proper course. Jane does not break the rule, because by luffing she is able to sail astern of Annie in position 3.

General limitations

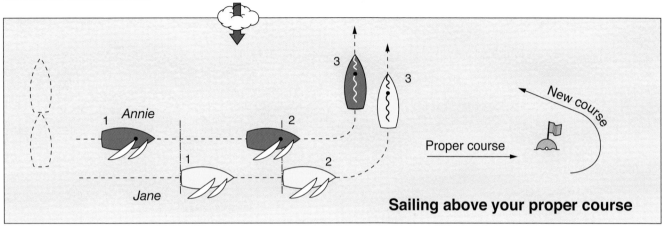

Sailing above your proper course

Comment

In position 1 Annie is clear astern, in position 2 Annie acquires an overlap to windward.

Jane may now sail higher than her course to the mark, i.e. above her proper course. Even as high as head to wind.

She may luff, but Annie must be able to take avoiding action without having to carry out daredevil feats.

So luffing is permitted, but not too quickly.

The difference with the situation on page 17 is **how** the overlap was created.

General limitations

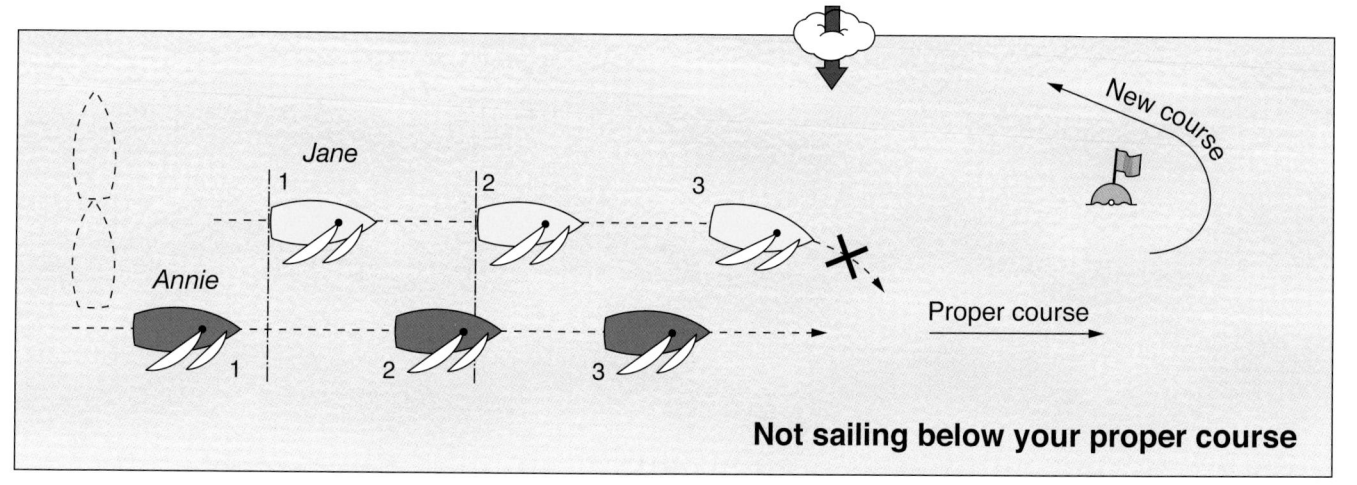

New course

Proper course

Not sailing below your proper course

17.2 On the same tack, proper course

Except on a beat to windward, while a boat is less than two of her hull lengths from a leeward boat or a boat clear astern steering a course to leeward of her, she shall not sail below her proper course unless... *(see next page).*

Comment

The distance between Annie and Jane is less than two hull lengths. In position 3, instead of sailing towards the mark, Jane sails a course to leeward of it, i.e. below her proper course.

Jane therefore breaks the rule.

General limitations

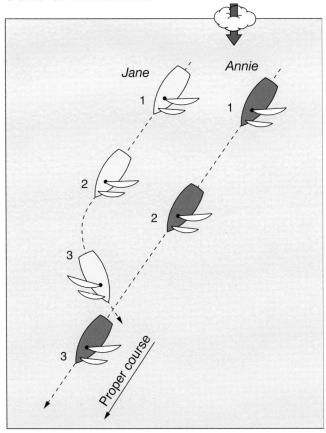

17.2 On the same tack, proper course

…unless she gybes.

Comment

In positions 1 and 2 Jane must not sail below her proper course. Jane does not break the rule, because by gybing in position 3 she is able to sail astern of Annie.

Starting

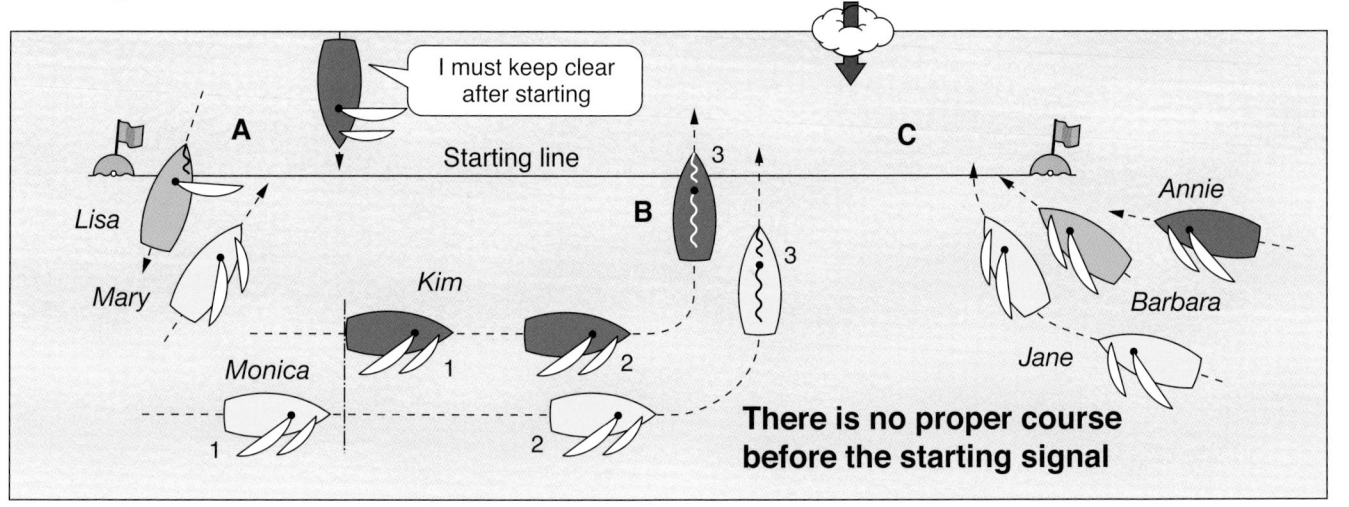

I must keep clear after starting

Starting line

There is no proper course before the starting signal

Lisa
Mary
Monica
Kim
Annie
Barbara
Jane

A
B
C

Now that we have learned some rules, here are a few situations that might occur *before* the start.

20 Sailing backwards

A boat moving astern by backing a sail shall keep clear of one that is not.

Comment

In situation A Lisa is backing her mainsail and starts to sail backwards. Lisa has to keep clear. In situation B Monica acquires an overlap to leeward and then starts to luff. Monica may luff up to head to wind, because there is no proper course before the starting signal.

In situation C Jane acquires an overlap to leeward. There is no proper course. Being a leeward boat she may luff and Annie and Barbara must get out. Rule 11 applies. Annie and Barbara are "barging".

At marks and obstructions

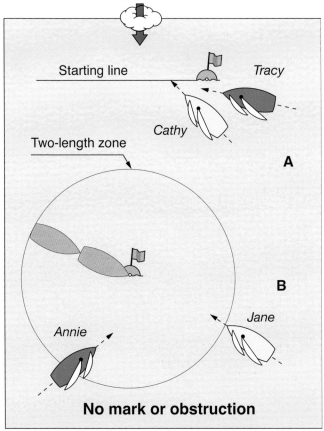

Starting line

Tracy

Cathy

A

Two-length zone

B

Jane

Annie

No mark or obstruction

18.1 Rounding and passing marks and obstructions

This rule applies at a mark or obstruction about to be rounded or passed.

However, it does not apply:
- At a starting mark surrounded by navigable water or at its anchor line.
- When boats are on opposite tacks and one of them has to tack to round the mark.

Comment

In situations A and B this rule does not apply.

In the top part of the illustration Tracy is barging, which is not permitted. Rule 11 applies here – the windward boat must keep clear of the leeward boat.

In the bottom part of the illustration rule 10 applies – the port-tack boat (Annie) must keep clear of the starboard-tack boat (Jane). In this case it does not matter whether the mark is there or not.

At marks and obstructions

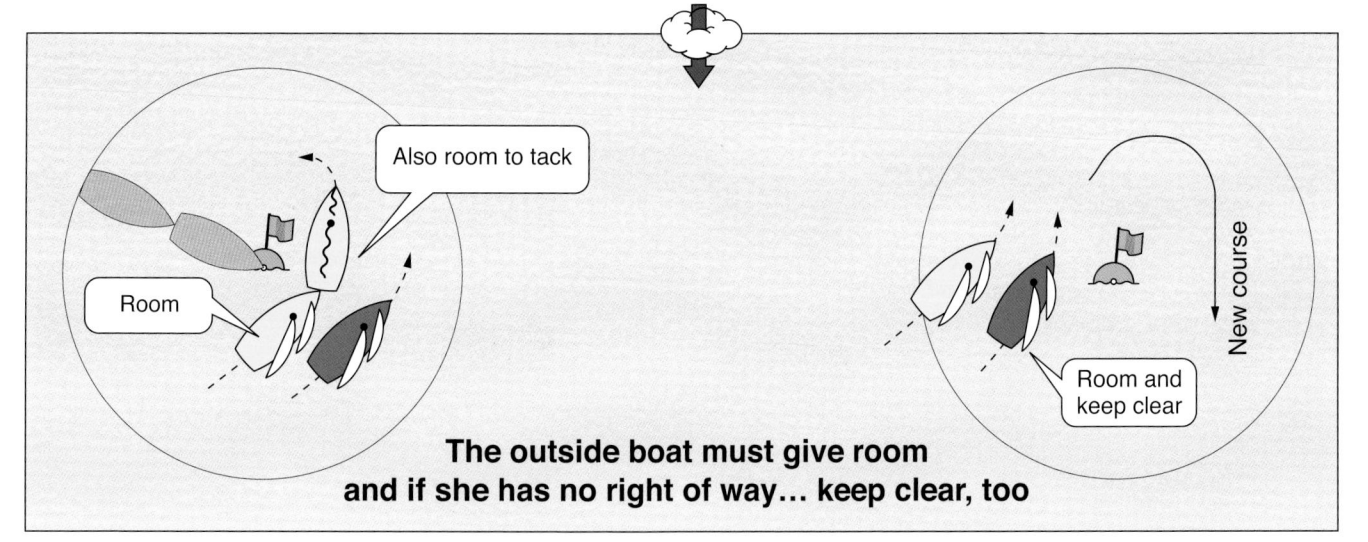

**The outside boat must give room
and if she has no right of way... keep clear, too**

18 Rounding and passing marks and obstructions

In rule 18 room means room for an inside boat to round or pass the mark or obstruction, including room to tack or gybe.

18.2 (a) Giving room; keeping clear
OVERLAPPED – BASIC RULE

When boats are overlapped the outside boat shall give the inside boat room to round or pass the mark or obstruction. If the inside boat has right of way the outside boat shall also keep clear.

At marks and obstructions

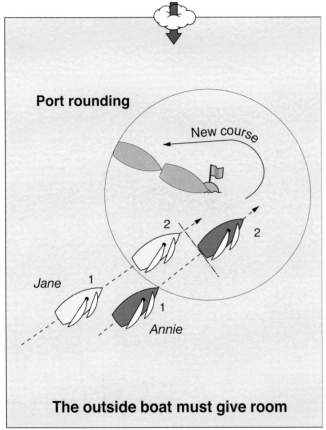

Port rounding

New course

2

Jane

1

2

1

Annie

The outside boat must give room

Rounding and passing marks and obstructions

18.2 (b) Giving room; keeping clear
OVERLAPPED AT THE ZONE

If boats were overlapped before either of them reached the two-length zone and the overlap is broken after one of them has reached it, the boat that was on the outside shall continue to give the other boat room.

Comment

In position 1 both boats are overlapped when the first boat reaches the two-length zone. Jane is the inside boat and must be given room to pass the mark. Since Annie as a leeward boat has right of way, she only needs to give room and Jane may not bear away to execute a nice, wide mark rounding, rule 11 – a windward boat must keep clear of a leeward boat.

In position 2 the overlap is broken. Nevertheless Annie must continue to give Jane room to round the mark.

At marks and obstructions

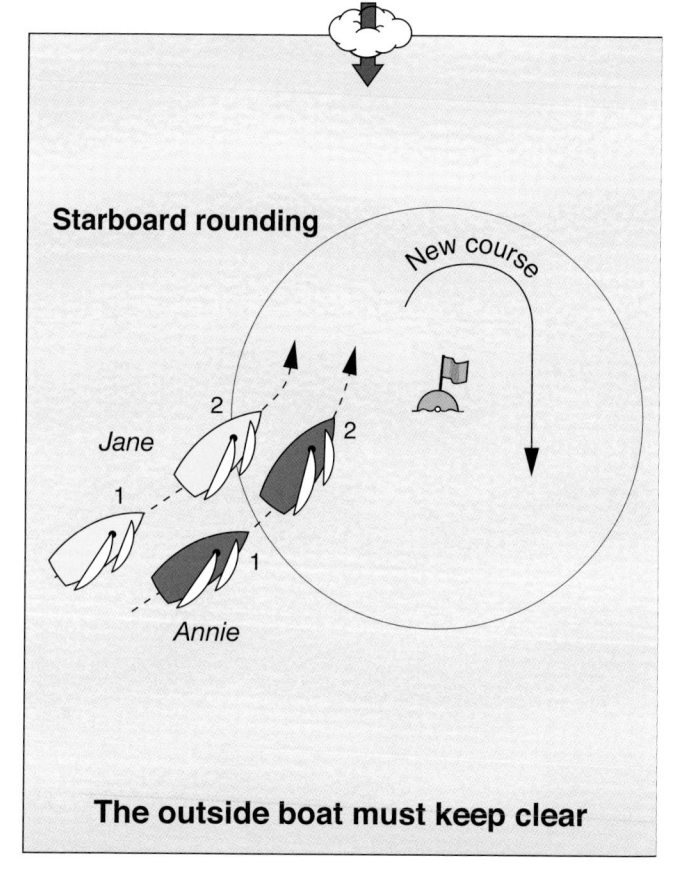

Starboard rounding

New course

2

Jane

2

1

1

Annie

The outside boat must keep clear

Rounding and passing marks and obstructions

18.2 (b) Giving room; keeping clear
OVERLAPPED AT THE ZONE

If boats were overlapped before either of them reached the two-length zone and the overlap is broken after one of them has reached it, the boat that was on the outside shall continue to give the other boat room.

Comment

In position 1 the boats are overlapped when they reach the two-length zone. Jane is the outside boat and must give room and keep clear of Annie. Since Annie as a leeward boat has right of way (rule 11 – a windward boat must keep clear of a leeward boat) , she may luff to execute a nice, wide (tactical) mark rounding,

Even if Jane later becomes the boat clear ahead, she is not entitled to room and must keep clear.

At marks and obstructions

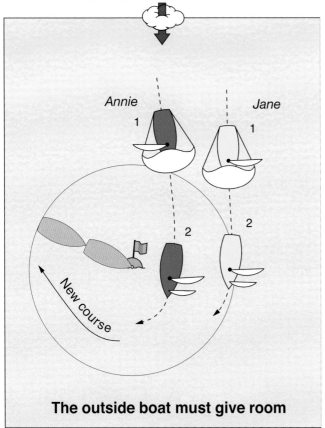

The outside boat must give room

Rounding and passing marks and obstructions

Comment

In position 1 Annie is sailing on port tack and Jane on starboard tack when Annie reaches the two-length zone. Under the basic rule Jane as an outside boat must give room, because they are overlapped when they reach the two-length zone.

Rule 10 – a boat on port tack must keep clear of a boat on starboard tack, does not apply here.

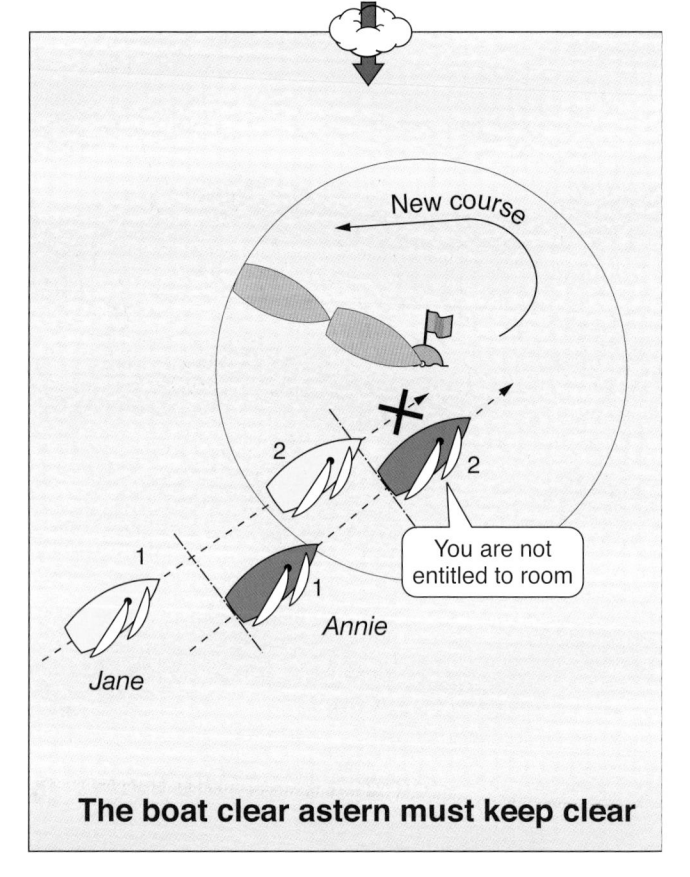

The boat clear astern must keep clear

Rounding and passing marks and obstructions

18.2 (c) Giving room; keeping clear
NOT OVERLAPPED AT THE ZONE

If a boat was clear ahead at the time she reached the two-length zone, the boat clear astern shall thereafter keep clear. If the boat clear astern becomes overlapped **inside** the other boat she is not entitled to room.

Comment

In position 1 Annie is clear ahead when she reaches the two-length zone. Jane must keep clear.

In position 2 an **inside** overlap has been established, but Jane is not entitled to room. In this situation she has to keep clear.

At marks and obstructions

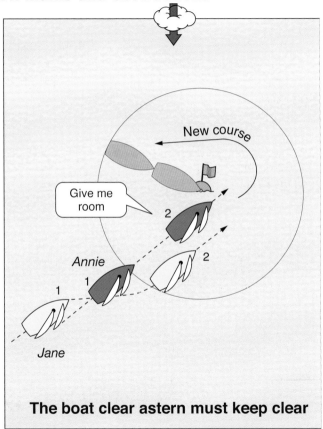

New course

Give me room

2

Annie

2

1

1

Jane

The boat clear astern must keep clear

Rounding and passing marks and obstructions

18.2 (c) Giving room; keeping clear
NOT OVERLAPPED AT THE ZONE

If a boat was clear ahead at the time she reached the two-length zone, the boat clear astern shall thereafter keep clear. If the boat clear astern becomes overlapped **outside** the other boat she shall also give the other boat room.

Comment

In position 1 Annie is clear ahead when she reaches the two-length zone. Jane must keep clear.

In position 2 an **outside** overlap has been established, but Jane must continue to keep clear, and she must also give room.

At marks and obstructions

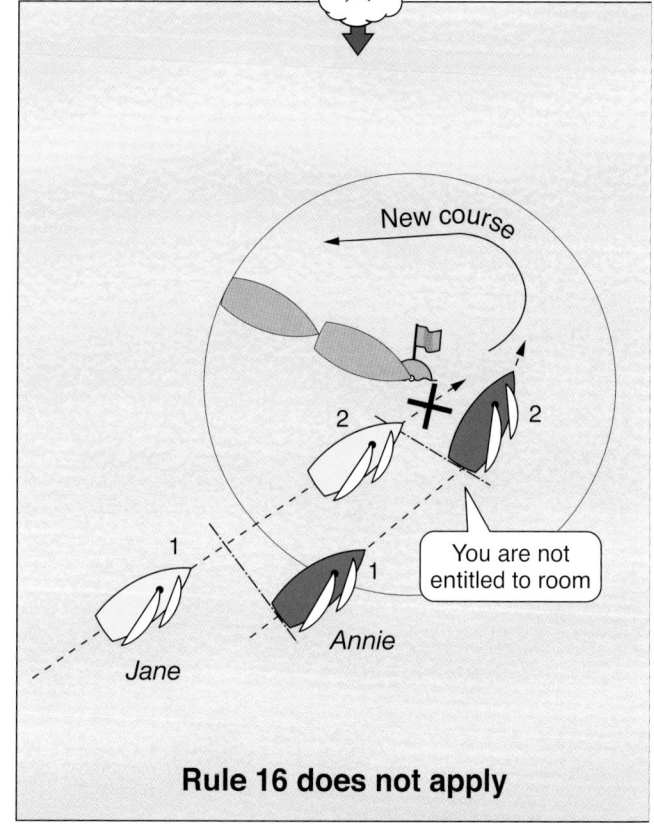

New course

2

2

1

You are not
entitled to room

1

Jane

Annie

Rule 16 does not apply

Rounding and passing marks and obstructions

18.2 (d) Giving room; keeping clear
CHANGING COURSE TO ROUND OR PASS

When, after the starting signal, rule 18 applies between two boats and the right-of-way boat is changing course to round or pass a mark, rule 16 does not apply.

Comment

In position 1 Annie is clear ahead when she reaches the two-length zone. Jane must keep clear.

In position 2 Annie changes course. Since rule 16 does not apply here, Jane is not entitled to room.

Rule 16
When a right-of-way boat changes course, she shall give the other boat room to keep clear.

At marks and obstructions

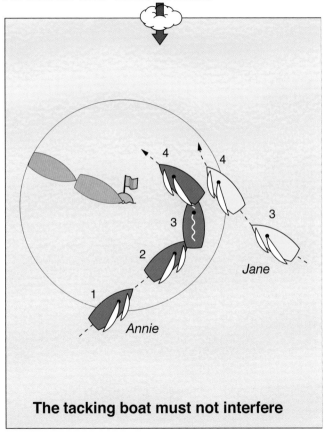

The tacking boat must not interfere

Rounding and passing marks and obstructions

18.3 (a) Tacking at a mark

If two boats were approaching a mark on opposite tacks and one of them completes a tack in the two-length zone when the other is fetching the mark, rule 18.2 does not apply.

The boat that tacked shall not cause the other boat to sail above close-hauled to avoid her, or prevent the other boat from passing the mark.

Comment

Annie is sailing on port tack and Jane is sailing on starboard tack (opposite tacks) when they approach the mark. Annie tacks inside the two-length zone, forcing Jane to sail above close-hauled. Annie breaks rule 18.3(a). The fact that Annie becomes the inside boat after her tacking manoeuvre makes no difference.

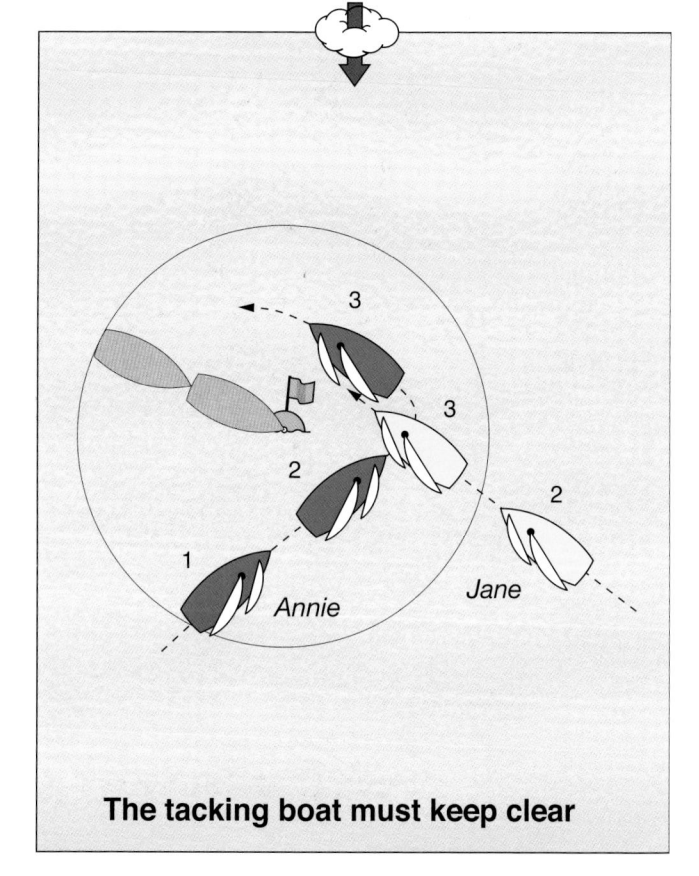

At marks and obstructions

The tacking boat must keep clear

Rounding and passing marks and obstructions

18.3 (b) Tacking at a mark

If two boats were approaching a mark on opposite tacks and one of them completes a tack in the two-length zone when the other is fetching the mark, rule 18.2 does not apply.

The boat that tacked shall give room if the other boat becomes overlapped inside her, in which case rule 15 – acquiring right of way – does not apply.

Comment

Annie is sailing on port tack and Jane is sailing on starboard tack (opposite tacks) when they enter the two-length zone. Annie tacks inside the zone. An overlap is then created and Jane cannot keep clear of Annie. Annie breaks rule 18.3(b).

  In practice this means that a boat that approaches a mark on port tack often takes a considerable risk.

At marks and obstructions

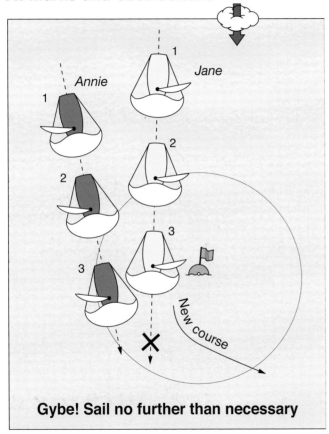

Gybe! Sail no further than necessary

Rounding and passing marks and obstructions

18.4 Gybing

When an inside overlapped right-of-way boat must gybe at a mark or obstruction to sail her proper course, until she gybes she shall sail no farther from the mark or obstruction than needed to sail that course.

Comment

Jane is sailing on starboard tack and has right of way. She is also the inside boat. In position 3 Jane may not sail farther than strictly necessary to adopt her new course. In this situation she must gybe as soon as possible after the mark.

At marks and obstructions

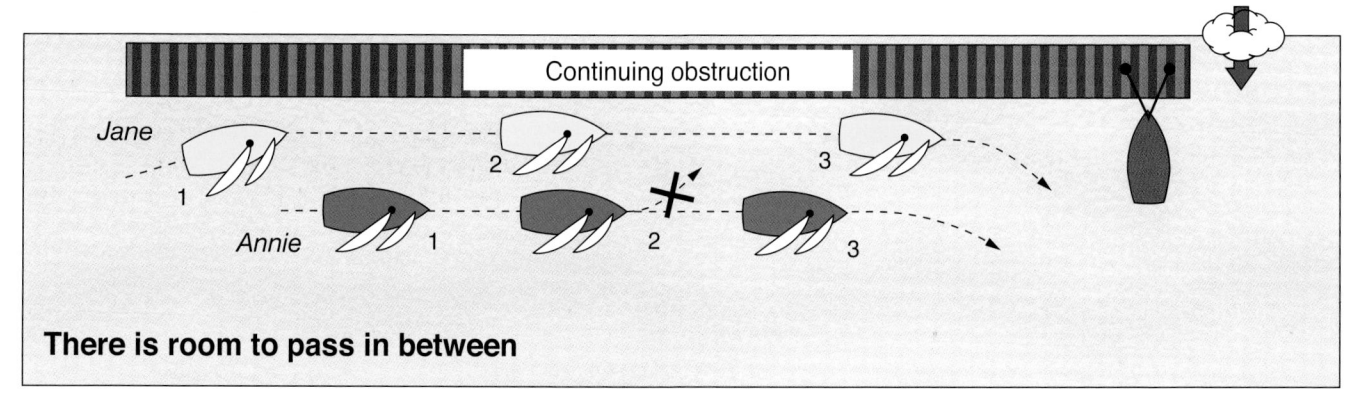

Continuing obstruction

Jane

Annie

There is room to pass in between

Rounding and passing marks and obstructions

18.5 Passing a continuing obstruction

While boats are passing a continuing obstruction, rules 18.2(b) and 18.2(c) do not apply.

A boat clear astern that obtains an inside overlap is entitled to room to pass between the other boat and the obstruction only if at the moment the overlap begins there is room to do so.

Comment

Position 1: Jane is clear astern of Annie while they are passing a continuing obstruction. Jane sees that there is sufficient space to pass between Annie and the continuing obstruction and decides to do so.

Position 2: Jane is sailing faster and passes to windward of Annie. From the moment the overlap is established Annie must give Jane room, even if she has to bear away later to avoid the obstruction – see position 3.

At marks and obstructions

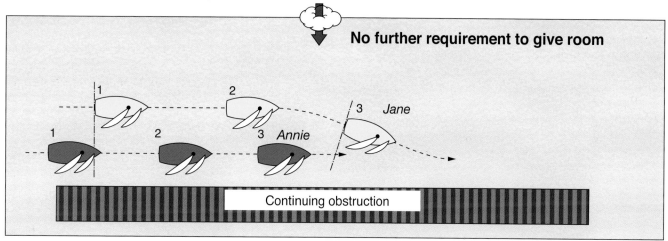

No further requirement to give room

Continuing obstruction

Comment

Position 1: Annie and Jane are passing a continuing
obstruction. They are overlapped.

Position 2: Jane is sailing faster and the overlap is
broken.

Position 3: Jane is no longer an outside boat, so she no
longer has to give room to Annie. Jane may
bear away.

At marks and obstructions

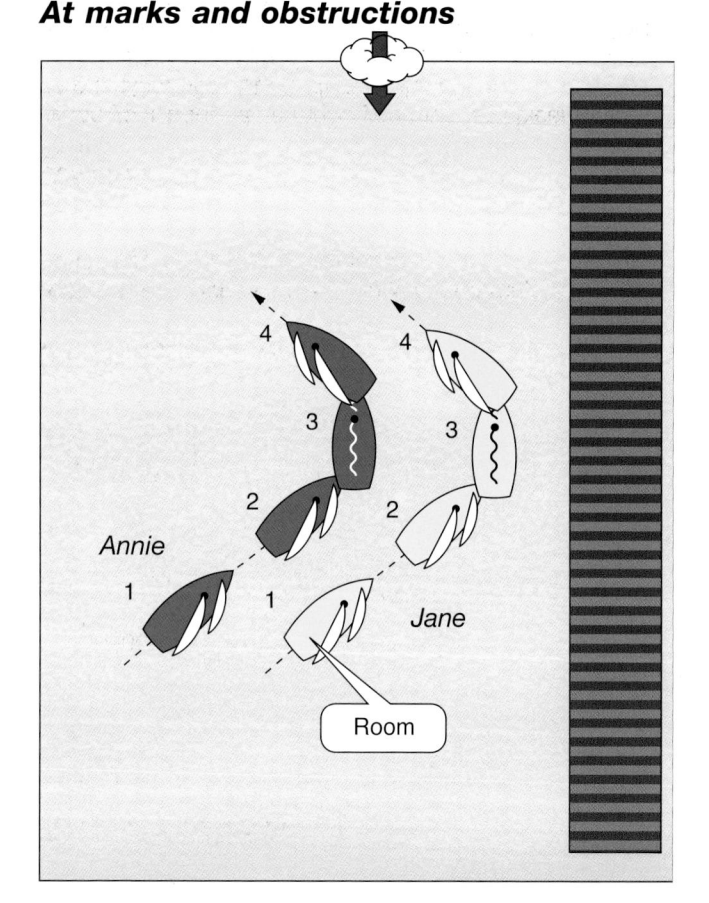

19 Room to tack at an obstruction

When safety requires a close-hauled boat to make a substantial course change to avoid an obstruction and she intends to tack, but cannot tack and avoid another boat on the same tack, she shall hail for **room** to do so. Before tacking she shall give the hailed boat time to respond.

The hailed boat shall respond by either:
a. tacking as soon as possible, or
b. promptly replying "You tack" and giving room to the hailing boat.

Comment

Position 1: Jane and Annie are sailing on port tack. Jane is approaching an obstruction and wants to tack, so she calls for "room" to do so.

Position 2: Annie must tack as soon as possible, and does so.

Then Jane, too, must tack as soon as possible.

Taking a penalty

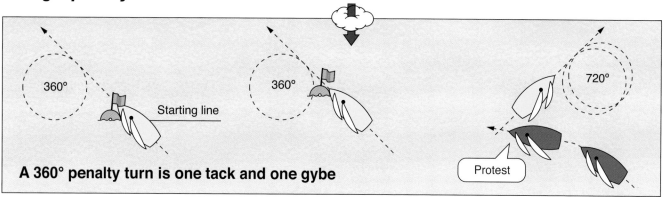

A 360° penalty turn is one tack and one gybe

31 Touching a mark

A boat that touches a mark while racing may take a penalty by making one turn (360°).

Comment

When your boat hits a mark, you must sail clear as soon as possible, without interfering with anyone, and immediately take your 360° penalty turn. If you hit the mark due to another boat's mistake, then that boat has to take a penalty turn.

44 Taking a penalty

A boat that breaks a rule against another boat must make two penalty turns (720°).

Comment

When you have broken a rule against another boat, in most cases you may continue racing, after sailing clear as soon as possible and taking two complete turns.
  When you touch a mark and you also break a rule, then two turns are sufficient.

Finishing

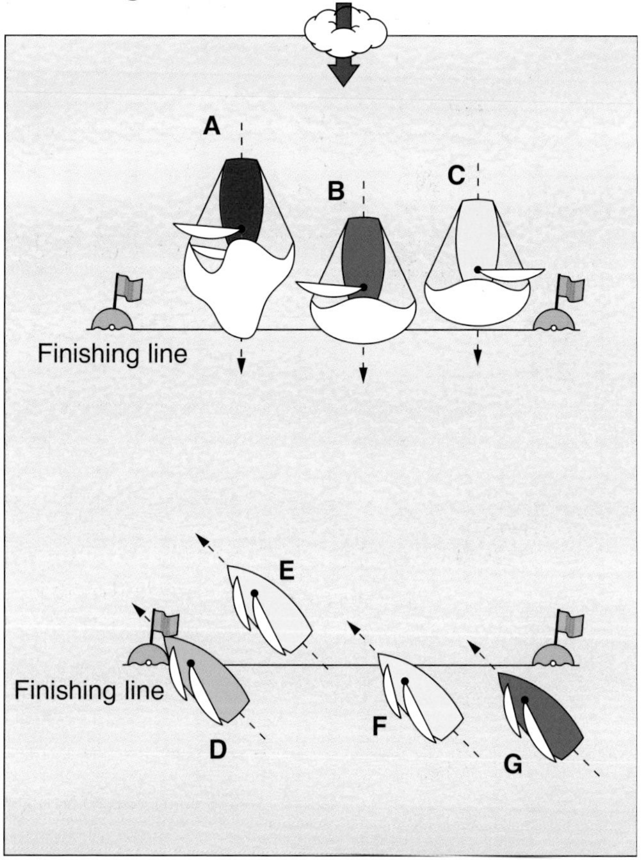

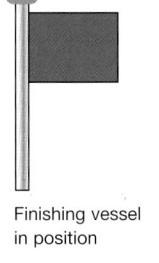

Definition

Finish

A boat finishes when any part of her hull, crew or equipment in normal position, crosses the finishing line in the direction of the course from the last mark.

Finishing vessel in position

Comment

A. Not yet finished, as the spinnaker is not in normal position.
B. Finished but still racing.
C. Not finished just yet.
D. Touched mark, then must take a penalty turn and subsequently finish again, the second finish counts.
E. Finished, and no longer racing.
F. Finished, but still racing.
G. Not finished just yet.

Finishing line

Finishing line

Finishing

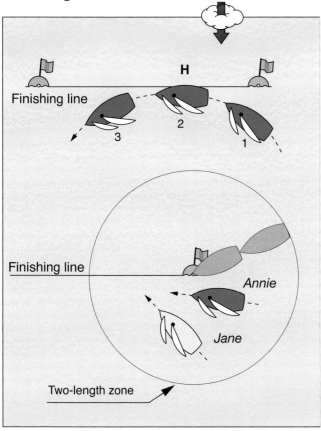

Finishing line

H

3

2

1

Finishing line

Annie

Jane

Two-length zone

Comment on top drawing

H. Position 2: finished but still racing.
   Position 3: finished and the race is over.

Comment on bottom drawing

At a finishing mark, unlike a mark at the starting line, the two-length zone applies. This means that all situations, from page 24 up to and including page 33, also apply to marks at the finishing line.

Assuming that Annie and Jane were overlapped when they entered the two-length zone, then Annie is entitled to room here.

If you have an outstanding penalty turn to take, you may do so after crossing the finishing line, but you must then return to the line to finish.
   The second time you cross the finishing line counts.

Protests

Protest

Describe the incident

Be honest and stick to the facts

* Boats with a hull length of less than 6 metres need not display a red flag.

Making a protest

Sailing is a sport without referees. When someone breaks a rule, it is up to you to take action. You must inform the other competitor of your intention to protest at the first reasonable opportunity. After the race you will have to lodge a written protest. A protest committee will then hear evidence from all the parties and give a decision.

This is what you have to do

A. At the first reasonable opportunity after the incident you shout "protest" and conspicuously display a red flag.* If the other boat is not within hailing distance, then notify him at the first opportunity.

B. Contact possible witnesses.

C. Get a protest form from the committee.

D. Fill out the form. The **incident** must be clearly described. *Any other details may be added or corrected during the hearing*.

E. Hand in the form before the end of the protest time limit.

F. Keep an eye on the official notice board to see when the protest committee will hear your protest.

G. Make sure that you and your witnesses, if any, are nearby until you are called.